INTEGRATIVE PSYCHIATRY APPROACHES

A Complete Guide On Exploring Holistic Healing And Harmonizing Mind And Body For Mental Well-Being

WALTER ZYAIRE

DISCLAIMER

The information in this book is intended only for general informational purposes; it should not be used in lieu of professional advice or medical care. Since the author is not licensed to practice therapy, the information offered should not be used in place of the expertise, judgment, or guidance of qualified mental health or medical professionals. Readers are encouraged to consult therapists, medical specialists, or other qualified authorities regarding their particular situation and needs. The publisher and author disclaim all liability for any actions or decisions taken by readers based on the information in this book. Results may vary from person to person and this book's approaches, procedures, and strategies may not be suitable in all circumstances. Considering unique situations and consulting a qualified expert are essential when choosing the right course of action. Neither the publisher nor the author recommend or guarantee the efficacy of any therapy or treatment that is indicated in this book. Because the information is based on the author's research and understanding at the time of publishing, it could not reflect the most recent developments or practices in the treatment area. The publisher and the author both disclaim all liability for the accuracy, completeness, or use of the material in this book. Readers bear full responsibility for the decisions and actions they choose in light of the information presented in this book.

TABLE OF CONTENTS

ABOUT THE BOOK

In the realm of mental health and healthcare, the book Integrative Psychiatry Approaches is highly influential. It provides a basic overview of integrative psychiatry in the introduction section, explaining its history, goals, and intended audience. This provides professionals and readers with a clear roadmap for the subsequent chapters and sets the stage for a thorough investigation of the subject matter.

The definition, guiding principles, and background of integrative psychiatry are explained in detail. The biopsychosocial model and holistic approaches to mental health are included to emphasize the discipline's multidimensionality. Before reading on to more complex subjects, this part gives readers a firm foundation in the fundamentals.

The book carefully breaks down the different facets of integrative psychiatry, beginning with its biological underpinnings. An extensive overview of the physiological foundations of integrative therapies is provided via the investigation of neurotransmitters, nutritional psychiatry, pharmaceutical interventions, and the role of genetics in mental health.

After that, psychological philosophies are discussed, including CBT, mindfulness, meditation, psychoanalysis, and expressive arts therapy. A full examination is given to social and environmental factors, such as family dynamics, cultural factors, and socioeconomic determinants. The content is further enhanced by the incorporation of lifestyle medicine, complementary and alternative therapies, and useful advice on incorporating these modalities into mental health procedures.

Integrative psychiatry in practice, ethical and legal issues, and future directions round out the book. Its practical application is increased by the inclusion of case studies, treatment planning, and collaborative care approaches. The ethical and legal aspects are thoroughly covered, guaranteeing that practitioners possess a solid comprehension of professional norms and legal structures. Finally, the book's forward-thinking approach is highlighted by the examination of future directions and developing research, which encourages professionals to stay up to date with developments in the field.

To put it simply, the book Integrative Psychiatry Approaches offers a thorough, organized resource that enables practitioners to use integrative psychiatry's many elements ethically and productively.

CHAPTER ONE

OVERVIEW OF INTEGRATIVE PSYCHIATRY APPROACHES

INTEGRATIVE PSYCHIATRY'S HISTORY

A broad, patient-centered approach to mental health care is encompassed by the dynamic and developing area of integrative psychiatry. Integrative psychiatry, which has its roots in the knowledge that mental health is a complex interplay of biological, psychological, and social elements, attempts to connect traditional and alternative modalities to meet the various requirements of individuals.

To achieve mental health and well-being, it is crucial to take the full person into account, as this holistic viewpoint emphasizes.

The origins of integrative psychiatry can be found in the increasing acknowledgment of the shortcomings of conventional psychiatric models. Traditional methods frequently overlook the complex nature of mental health and the larger context of an individual's life in favor of pharmacological interventions that regulate symptoms. In response to this constraint, integrative psychiatry is born, focusing on a more individualized and inclusive treatment strategy that incorporates a range of therapeutic methods.

INTEGRATIVE PSYCHIATRY'S BASICS

Integrative psychiatry's basic tenet is the recognition that biological, psychological, and social variables all have an impact on mental health. One of the main ideas of integrative psychiatry, the Biopsychosocial Model, is based on the connections between these aspects. According to this concept, psychological experiences, social and environmental circumstances, and biological processes interact to produce mental health and sickness. Taking into account this complex network of effects, integrative psychiatry practitioners' work to customize interventions to meet the distinctive needs of each patient.

The concept of cooperation and synergy between various therapy modalities is at the core of integrative psychiatry's definition and guiding principles. Instead of rigidly following a single approach, practitioners include evidence-based methods from a variety of fields, such as alternative therapies, psychotherapy, traditional psychiatry, nutritional interventions, and mindfulness. Integrative psychiatry's guiding principles emphasize the value of a patient-centered strategy, individualized treatment programs, and a dedication to treating mental health issues at their source.

AN OVERVIEW OF THE PAST

An examination of the field's past shows how integrative psychiatry has gradually changed to adapt to the evolving demands of mental health treatment. A more comprehensive knowledge of mental health has gained traction in recent decades, driven by developments in psychology and neuroscience as well as the growing acceptance of complementary and alternative therapies. The reductionist perspective of mental health has given way to a more integrated and comprehensive viewpoint, which is reflected in integrative psychiatry.

ALL-ENCOMPASSING METHODS FOR MENTAL HEALTH

Integrative psychiatry's foundational ideas center on holistic approaches to mental wellness. This entails realizing that mental health is dependent on a wider range of variables than only the absence of symptoms, such as lifestyle, diet, stress management, and interpersonal interactions. Dietary adjustments, physical activity, mindfulness exercises, and other lifestyle adjustments that support a more resilient and balanced mental state can all be included in holistic therapies.

Integrative Psychiatry acknowledges the intricate interactions between biological, psychological, and social elements, marking a paradigm shift in the treatment of mental illness. This method, which is based on the Biopsychosocial Model, places a strong emphasis on teamwork, individualized treatment plans, and an all-encompassing perspective on mental health. Integrative psychiatry has the potential to provide more thorough and customized answers to the problems associated with mental health as the profession develops.

CHAPTER TWO

FOUNDATIONS IN BIOLOGY

PSYCHIATRIC DISORDERS AND NEUROTRANSMITTERS

Understanding the complex relationship between neurotransmitters and psychiatric diseases is fundamental to comprehending the physiological underpinnings of mental health. The chemical messengers known as neurotransmitters, which let neurons communicate with one another, are essential for controlling behavior, mood, and thought processes. Neurotransmitter imbalances, including those involving serotonin, dopamine, and norepinephrine, are often linked to several mental illnesses.

For example, anomalies in dopamine function are linked to schizophrenia and several mood disorders, whereas disturbances in serotonin transmission are linked to illnesses like anxiety and sadness.

DIETARY PSYCHIATRY

The growing discipline of nutritional psychiatry emphasizes how important nutrition is for mental health. Studies show that eating habits can affect the synthesis of neurotransmitters, synaptic function, and inflammation—all of which are linked to mental illnesses. Antioxidants, omega-3 fatty acids, and specific vitamins and minerals have been linked to a decreased incidence of depression and other mental health issues in diets high in these nutrients. On the other hand, diets heavy in sugar, processed foods, and saturated fats may make people more susceptible to mental health issues. Given the complex relationship between nutrition and mental health, it is critical to take nutritional interventions into account while providing all-encompassing mental health care.

DRUG-RELATED INTERVENTIONS

For a considerable amount of time, the foundation of care for mental illnesses has consisted of pharmaceutical interventions. Neurotransmitter systems are the focus of psychotropic drugs including anxiolytics, antidepressants, and antipsychotics, which aim to reduce symptoms and enhance mental health in general. These drugs work by adjusting the amounts or activities of particular neurotransmitters in the brain. Although many people have found pharmacological therapies to be effective, researchers are always looking for new substances and ways to improve treatment outcomes while reducing side effects. Furthermore, the requirement for individualized treatment strategies based on each patient's distinct neurochemistry and symptomatology is highlighted by the personalized character of pharmacology.

MENTAL HEALTH AND GENETICS

Research on the complex and ever-evolving relationship between genetics and mental health is underway. Genetic predispositions are a significant influence in the development of psychiatric diseases, even though environmental factors also play a role.

Studies including families and twins have consistently shown that disorders like major depressive disorder, bipolar disorder, and schizophrenia have a heritable component. Thanks to developments in molecular genetics and genomics, several genetic variants have been linked to a higher risk of mental health issues. In addition to providing information for risk assessment, knowing the genetic foundation of mental health holds promise for the development of focused therapy strategies that target the underlying biological mechanisms causing these diseases.

CHAPTER THREE

METHODS OF PSYCHOLOGY

CBT, OR COGNITIVE-BEHAVIORAL THERAPY

The psychological technique known as cognitive-behavioral therapy (CBT) is popular and focuses on the interaction of ideas, emotions, and behaviors. The basic idea of cognitive behavioral therapy (CBT) is that our ideas affect our emotions, which in turn affect our actions. CBT seeks to reduce psychological suffering by identifying and altering problematic thought patterns and behaviors. Together, therapists and clients confront unfavorable thought patterns, swap them out for realistic and upbeat ones, and create more beneficial coping techniques. This method works very well for treating depression, anxiety disorders, and different types of phobias. CBT aims to provide people with the self-awareness and useful skills they need to better control their emotions and behaviors.

MEDITATION & MINDFULNESS

The contemplative techniques of mindfulness and meditation have their roots in Eastern philosophy and have become increasingly popular in Western psychology. Cultivating awareness of the current moment without passing judgment is a component of mindfulness. The goal of meditation techniques like loving-kindness or focused attention is to improve mindfulness.

These strategies have been included in several therapeutic therapies to lower stress, sharpen attention, and promote general well-being. Studies indicate that mindfulness-based therapy may be helpful in the treatment of illnesses like depression, anxiety, and chronic pain. A more compassionate and balanced relationship with one's inner experiences can be developed by encouraging a nonjudgmental awareness of one's thoughts and feelings.

INTEGRATION OF PSYCHIATRY AND PSYCHOANALYSIS

Sigmund Freud created psychoanalysis, a thorough psychological method that examines the unconscious mind and how early events affect present-day actions and interpersonal interactions. It places a strong emphasis on how the unconscious, early experiences, and the id, ego, and superego shape personality. Integrative psychiatry addresses the biological, psychological, and social facets of mental health by fusing conventional psychiatric therapies with complementary and alternative methods. This all-encompassing method acknowledges the connections between many elements that affect mental health. Integrative psychiatry frequently combines therapeutic modalities, including medication, lifestyle modifications, psychotherapy, and nutritional support, to develop a customized treatment plan that meets each patient's specific requirements.

THERAPEUTIC EXPRESSIVE ARTS

A creative and all-encompassing method, expressive arts therapy employs a variety of artistic mediums to facilitate self-expression and inquiry. It consists of poetry, dance, music, theatre, and visual arts to aid in emotional processing and communication. This therapy approach acknowledges the role that creativity plays in fostering recovery and personal development.

People can access and release feelings through artistic expression that may be difficult to convey verbally. Trauma, anxiety, and despair are just a few of the mental health conditions that are treated by expressive arts therapy. The process itself—which promotes self-discovery and emotional well-being via creative exploration—is prioritized over the artistic result.

CHAPTER FOUR

ENVIRONMENTAL AND SOCIAL FACTORS

SOCIAL DETERMINANTS OF MENTAL HEALTH

These variables go beyond the conventional emphasis on biological and psychological elements to include a wide variety of elements that affect a person's mental health. These factors have their origins in the social and economic environments in which individuals are created, develop, live, work, and age.

A person's home situation, education, career prospects, socioeconomic level, and ease of access to healthcare services are all important factors that influence their mental health. Differential mental health outcomes can arise from disparities in these social factors, underscoring the necessity of an all-encompassing and inclusive approach to mental health care that takes the larger social environment into account.

CULTURAL ASPECTS

People's perceptions, experiences, and expressions of mental health issues are greatly influenced by their culture. Cultural factors in mental health refer to the various belief systems, values, customs, and behaviors that influence how particular groups see and handle mental health concerns. In mental health care, cultural competence entails acknowledging and honoring these varied viewpoints, modifying interventions to conform to cultural norms, and encouraging candid dialogue. Ignorance of cultural influences may result in incorrect diagnosis, stigma, and inadequate care. Therefore, to guarantee that mental health services are relevant and accessible to people from diverse cultural backgrounds, a culturally sensitive approach is important.

FAMILY AND COMMUNITY SUPPORT

These networks play a critical role in fostering mental health and overall well-being. Families are an important part of a person's mental health journey since they are the main providers of emotional, social, and practical support. Cohesion, communication, and positive family dynamics all support resilience and improved mental health outcomes. In addition, a protective atmosphere that promotes mental health is created by community support, which includes friendships, social networks, and community services. However, social exclusion and a lack of assistance can make mental health problems worse. Creating comprehensive mental health initiatives requires acknowledging and valuing the relationships that people have with their families and communities.

INTEGRATIVE PSYCHIATRY IN DIVERSE CONTEXTS

Integrative psychiatry is a strategy that integrates complementary and alternative therapies with traditional psychiatric treatments to address mental health issues holistically. This method acknowledges the relationship between social, mental, and physical health.

There are several contexts in which integrative psychiatry can be used, such as clinics, hospitals, and community-based initiatives. More individualized and comprehensive approaches to mental health care are made possible by combining traditional psychiatric therapies with practices like mindfulness, yoga, nutritional interventions, and psychotherapy. Interventions that are customized to each patient's requirements and preferences improve therapeutic efficacy and promote general well-being. The amalgamation of many therapy modalities signifies a transition towards a mental care model that is more inclusive and patient-centered.

CHAPTER FIVE

ALTERNATIVE AND COMPLEMENTARY MEDICINE

HERBAL MEDICINE

Often referred to as botanical medicine, herbal medicine is an alternative and complementary therapy that uses plants and plant extracts for therapeutic effects. This method, which draws on the therapeutic qualities of herbs to treat a variety of medical ailments, has been used for ages in many different civilizations. Herbal medicines can be made into teas, tinctures, capsules, topical applications, or other forms. Frequently, they are made from leaves, roots, stems, flowers, or seeds. Herbal medicine proponents claim that a wide range of substances found in plants has medicinal properties and, when utilized correctly, can aid in the body's natural healing processes. Despite the lengthy history of herbal therapy, it is important to use caution while using it because it may combine with conventional pharmaceuticals or have unintended adverse effects.

ACUPUNCTURE AND TRADITIONAL CHINESE MEDICINE

These age-old medical techniques have developed in China over thousands of years as part of Traditional Chinese Medicine (TCM). According to TCM principles, acupuncture involves inserting tiny needles into particular body sites to promote Qi or energy flow. It is thought that this exercise will balance the body's essential energy and enhance general health. A holistic approach is used in traditional Chinese medicine, which includes food therapy, herbal medicine, acupuncture, and activities like Tai Chi.

According to TCM, sickness results from disturbances in the harmonic balance between the Yin and Yang forces, which is seen as the basis for health. In Western medicine, acupuncture and other TCM methods are becoming more widely recognized as supplementary therapies for a range of ailments, such as pain treatment, stress reduction, and enhancing general energy flow.

Both yoga and tai chi are mind-body exercises that have their roots in ancient cultures and are popular supplementary and alternative therapies today. Yoga is a physical and mental health practice that originated in ancient India. It incorporates physical postures, breath control, meditation, and ethical concepts. It is well-recognized that the practice improves strength, relaxation, and flexibility. Tai Chi is a kind of Chinese martial art that emphasizes deep breathing, slow, deliberate motions, and meditation. The possible benefits of yoga and tai chi include stress reduction, balance improvement, and general physical and mental health enhancement. Due to their accessibility and holistic approach to wellness maintenance, these techniques have become more and more popular in Western cultures.

ENERGY HEALING MODALITIES

These are a broad category of techniques that aim to influence the body's energy fields to facilitate healing. These methods are based on the idea that illness or discomfort might result from imbalances or interruptions in the body's energy. Energy manipulation or channeling is used by practitioners of techniques like Reiki, Healing Touch, and Qigong to promote the body's inherent healing capacities and restore equilibrium. Proponents of energy healing contend that by encouraging relaxation, lowering stress levels, and enhancing general well-being, it can supplement conventional medicine—even if the scientific validity of these methods is up for question. For a thorough approach to health and healing, like with any supplementary therapy, it is crucial to approach energy healing with an open mind and seek advice from medical authorities.

CHAPTER SIX

LIFESTYLE MEDICINE

FOOD AND NUTRITIONAL THERAPIES

A comprehensive approach to health is included in lifestyle medicine, which acknowledges the significant influence of lifestyle decisions on general well-being. This paradigm emphasizes the importance of nutrition and dietary treatments and recognizes that the food we eat has a direct impact on our health. Maintaining optimal body functions, preventing chronic diseases, and boosting longevity all depend on eating a nutritious, well-balanced diet. Achieving and maintaining excellent health requires a focus on the eating of whole, unprocessed foods and absorbing a variety of elements, including vitamins, minerals, and antioxidants. Individualized dietary therapies can be very effective in treating disorders such as diabetes, obesity, and heart disease.

PHYSICAL ACTIVITY AND EXERCISE

The importance of physical activity and exercise in lifestyle medicine is another. Frequent physical activity has been linked to many health advantages, such as better cardiovascular health, improved mental health, and easier weight management. Including aerobic and strength-training exercises in daily routines promotes overall vitality, helps maintain a healthy body weight, and develops muscles and bones. In addition to being a preventative strategy against chronic diseases, physical activity is essential for managing them. Individualized fitness regimens that are tailored to each person's capabilities and preferences are essential elements of Lifestyle Medicine treatments.

HYGIENE OF SLEEP

Keeping a healthy lifestyle requires good sleep hygiene, which is something that is frequently disregarded. For cognitive performance, emotional stability, and physical and mental recovery, adequate and high-quality sleep is crucial. The field of lifestyle medicine places significant emphasis on the establishment of regular sleep habits, the creation of a sleep-friendly environment, and the adoption of relaxation-promoting practices before bedtime. Improving sleep hygiene and treating sleep problems have a good impact on conditions including anxiety, depression, and metabolic diseases in addition to being very beneficial to general health.

DRUG ABUSE AND USE

Abuse and misuse of substances pose serious risks to one's general health and well-being. The field of lifestyle medicine recognizes the detrimental impacts that alcohol, tobacco, and illegal drug use have on different organ systems. Interventions in this area focus on preventative and harm-reduction techniques in addition to treating addiction-related problems. To effectively treat substance use disorders, lifestyle medicine acknowledges the significance of comprehensive therapies that include behavioral, psychological, and social elements. Support, information, and assistance for those battling addiction are essential components of Lifestyle Medicine's larger concept.

 Lifestyle medicine takes a holistic and personalized approach to health, emphasizing the connections between sleep, exercise, diet, and substance abuse. By addressing these factors, professionals hope to enable people to adopt lasting lifestyle modifications that will improve long-term health and stop the development or progression of chronic illnesses.

CHAPTER SEVEN

CASE STUDIES

INTEGRATIVE PSYCHIATRY IN PRACTICE

Within the field of Integrative Psychiatry, case studies are a vital resource that helps practitioners gain a deeper comprehension of customized treatment plans. These real-world examples provide a sophisticated viewpoint on the intricacies of mental health, enabling medical professionals to investigate the complicated nature of psychiatric disorders.

Case studies offer a means of integrating different therapy modalities while taking into account the biological, emotional, and environmental variables that all play a part in a patient's overall health. Practitioners can improve their diagnostic abilities and customize interventions to meet the particular needs of each patient by focusing on particular instances.

TREATMENT PLANNING

Integrative psychiatry places a strong emphasis on a comprehensive approach to mental health care through a dynamic and collaborative treatment planning process. To attain complete well-being, it entails combining complementary and alternative therapies with traditional psychiatric treatments. An extensive evaluation of the patient's medical background, psychological symptoms, and lifestyle choices is the first step in the process.

Using this data, medical professionals can create a customized treatment plan that might incorporate medication, nutritional therapies, mindfulness exercises, psychotherapy, and other approaches. Making a road plan that takes into account a person's physical, emotional, and spiritual needs will help them regain their mental health in a way that is sustainable and well-balanced.

COLLABORATIVE CARE MODELS

Integrative psychiatry's practical success is largely dependent on collaborative care models. These models place a strong emphasis on working as a team, bringing together primary care physicians, psychiatrists, psychologists, dietitians, and other medical specialists to address the various needs of their patients. To guarantee that treatment plans are thorough and well-coordinated, team members must communicate and work together effectively. With its focus on treating the complete person, integrative psychiatry stands to gain a great deal from collaborative care models that make it easier to combine complementary and conventional therapy. This multidisciplinary method encourages a patient-centered approach to mental health care and increases the efficacy of interventions.

OPPORTUNITIES AND DIFFICULTIES

Although integrative psychiatry offers a potential strategy for treating mental illness, there are drawbacks. The need for greater understanding and acceptance from the mainstream medical community is one of the main obstacles. Establishing credibility and evidence-based methods necessitates continual education and cooperation to bridge the gap between traditional and integrative techniques.

Furthermore, some people may be skeptical about the incorporation of complementary therapies, thus a well-rounded and evidence-based strategy is required.

Notwithstanding these obstacles, there exist noteworthy prospects for ingenuity and enhancement in the provision of mental healthcare services. More therapeutic alternatives are available in integrative psychiatry, which honors patient preferences and encourages active patient participation in treatment. The increasing amount of evidence demonstrating the effectiveness of integrative methods offers a chance for the field to become more widely recognized. Additionally, telemedicine and technological developments provide new ways to provide integrative mental health care, removing constraints related to location and improving accessibility for a wider range of patients. By seizing these chances, Integrative Psychiatry can advance in the field of mental health treatment and provide a more individualized and inclusive approach to well-being.

CHAPTER EIGHT

LEGAL AND ETHICAL ISSUES TO CONSIDER

KNOWLEDGEABLE CONSENT

The informed consent concept is a fundamental aspect of ethical and legal issues in the healthcare industry. The ethical duty to guarantee that people are fully informed about any medical operation, treatment, or intervention before giving their assent is included in informed consent. This idea emphasizes how important it is to respect patients' autonomy and give them the tools they need to make wise healthcare decisions.

To promote a cooperative and courteous relationship based on openness and trust, practitioners must provide pertinent information, including potential risks and advantages, in a way that is understandable to the patient.

Another essential ethical principle that serves as the cornerstone of patient-provider interaction is confidentiality. Maintaining patient privacy and creating the sense of security needed for candid and open discussion depend on maintaining confidentiality. The confidentiality of patient information is a legal and ethical requirement for healthcare workers. This involves safeguarding private information exchanged in medical records, consultations, and other correspondence. The seriousness of this ethical issue in healthcare practice is highlighted by the fact that breaches of confidentiality not only damage confidence but may also have legal repercussions.

INTEGRATIVE PSYCHIATRY AND ETHICS IN THE WORKPLACE

A distinct set of ethical issues is introduced by integrative psychiatry, a holistic approach that blends traditional and complementary therapies, particularly when considering professional standards. When integrating several therapy methods, practitioners who embrace integrative psychiatry must follow the established norms and criteria of their respective professions. To maintain patient safety, efficacious treatment, and professional reputation, it is imperative to maintain a delicate equilibrium between innovation and established standards. Integrative psychiatry's ethical concerns include open communication regarding non-conventional methods, supporting patients' freedom to select their treatment options, and regularly assessing the security and effectiveness of integrative therapy.

CONCERNS WITH LAW AND REGULATION

The intricacy of ethical considerations in healthcare is further compounded by legal and regulatory issues. The legal and ethical landscape is complex, and practitioners need to stay on top of it to maintain their legal and ethical standing. This entails being aware of the prerequisites for licensure, keeping up with changes in healthcare legislation, and abiding by professional standards of behavior. In addition to endangering the practitioner's career, noncompliance with legal and regulatory frameworks compromises the integrity of the healthcare system. In this situation, making ethical decisions requires a dedication to maintaining patient and community welfare as well as legal literacy and ethical contemplation.

It is critical to uphold the integrity of the healthcare profession that ethical and legal considerations are intertwined. The value of patient autonomy and privacy is emphasized by informed consent and confidentiality, and integrative psychiatry demands a careful balancing act between new ideas and accepted professional norms. When it comes to navigating legal and regulatory difficulties, healthcare providers need to be alert, knowledgeable, and dedicated to honoring their legal obligations as well as their ethical standards.

CHAPTER NINE

FUTURE PATHS

EMERGING RESEARCH IN INTEGRATIVE PSYCHIATRY

The field of integrative psychiatry is always changing due to new research that explores the complex relationships between the environment, body, and mind. The potential of cutting-edge therapeutic approaches, such as psychedelic-assisted therapy, to treat a range of mental health issues has been investigated in recent studies.

These methods are leading the way for novel treatment approaches and expanding our understanding of the neurological bases of psychiatric diseases. Furthermore, studies are illuminating the function of genetics, epigenetic, and the microbiome in mental health, providing a more thorough viewpoint on customized treatment.

THE RELATIONSHIP BETWEEN TECHNOLOGY AND MENTAL HEALTH

Integrative psychiatry is not an exception to the new age of mental health treatment brought about by technological advancements. With the rise in popularity of telepsychiatry, patients can now receive mental health services from a distance. Sensor-equipped wearables and mobile applications can offer useful information for tracking and treating mental health issues.

With the ability to provide individualized therapies based on each patient's profile, artificial intelligence (AI) is also making major advancements in supporting diagnostic and therapy planning. Nonetheless, when integrating technology into psychiatric practice, ethical issues, privacy concerns, and the digital divide continue to be crucial factors that require careful study.

As integrative psychiatry develops globally, it acknowledges the various cultural, social, and economic determinants that impact mental health. An increasingly essential component of global mental health is the integration of indigenous knowledge and traditional healing techniques into psychiatric therapy. Investigating the efficacy and acceptability of diverse interventions among diverse groups is the goal of cross-cultural research. To create inclusive and culturally sensitive approaches and recognize that mental health is a global issue with regional variations in expression and treatment, international collaboration is important.

THE INTEGRATIVE PSYCHIATRIST'S CHANGING ROLE

Future integrative psychiatrists are managing a changing environment and taking a more comprehensive approach than just treating symptoms.

This means taking into account lifestyle factors, social determinants, and environmental impacts in addition to the biological aspects of mental health. Psychiatry and other healthcare disciplines are increasingly being integrated through the use of multidisciplinary teams in collaborative care models. Moreover, integrative psychiatrists advocate for policy modifications, community involvement, and destigmatization initiatives outside of the clinical context. In line with the goal of complete well-being for people and communities, the focus is moving from reactive treatment to proactive mental health promotion and prevention.